INSIDE THE WORLD'S MOST FAMOUS INTELLIGENCE AGENCIES

Inside America's CIA

The Central Intelligence Agency

Janet Hines

The Rosen Publishing Group, Inc.
New York

Published in 2003 by The Rosen Publishing Group, Inc.
29 East 21st Street, New York, NY 10010

First Edition

Library of Congress Cataloging-in-Publication Data

Hines, Janet.
Inside America's CIA: the Central Intelligence Agency/by Janet Hines.—1st ed.
p. cm.—(Inside the world's most famous intelligence agencies)
Summary: Presents the United States Central Intelligence Agency (CIA) as having evolved from its maverick days during the Cold War to become a major player in the war against terrorism.
Includes bibliographical references and index.
ISBN 0-8239-3811-5 (library binding)
1. United States. Central Intelligence Agency—Juvenile literature.
[1. United States. Central Intelligence Agency. 2. Intelligence service. 3. Espionage.]
I. Title. II. Series.
UB251.U5 H55 2003
327.1273—dc21

2002012249

Manufactured in the United States of America

Cover image: CIA headquarters, located about eight miles from downtown Washington in Langley, Virginia. The original buildings and grounds, completed in 1963, were conceived by then director of central intelligence Allen W. Dulles to reflect the atmosphere of a college campus. The addition, known as The New Headquarters, opened in 1991.

INSIDE THE WORLD'S MOST FAMOUS INTELLIGENCE AGENCIES

Contents

Introduction

The United States has existed for more than 200 years. Located in North America, sandwiched between Canada and Mexico, the United States has a population of 280,000,000 people and is under the leadership of a democratic government.

It was on July 4, 1776, that the American colonies, part of the British Empire, declared independence from King George III. For the next seven years, the colonies were embroiled in a bitter war with their former ruler until winning their independence in 1783.

Today, the United States government is made up of the office of the president, the Senate, and the House of Representatives. At this writing, George W. Bush, son of former president George H. W. Bush, is the nation's forty-third president. Before becoming president, George Bush had been governor of Texas for six years.

Intelligence gathering in America is still young. The United States first gathered intelligence during times of war under the direction of the military. For much of the country's history, however, there has been no agency to gather intelligence during peacetime.

In 1945, after World War II, the country's attention shifted from wartime enemies Nazi Germany, Japan, and Italy to the threat of Communism, a style of government very different from America's democracy. America's leaders saw

After the terrorist attacks in the United States on September 11, 2001, President George W. Bush announced that the country would undertake a war on terrorism. The immediate goal was to hunt down Osama bin Laden, the man considered responsible for organizing the brutal event, as well as his followers, believed to be hiding in the mountains of Afghanistan. As of this writing, the CIA believes that bin Laden is still hiding in the mountains and traveling by horseback to avoid detection. Others believe he has died.

a need to establish an intelligence agency to monitor Communist governments as they spread throughout Europe, guided by the Soviet Union.

In September 1947, President Harry Truman signed the National Security Act, creating the Central Intelligence Agency (CIA), America's new national intelligence organization. The National Security Act also established the National Security Agency (NSA), the Defense Intelligence Agency (DIA), and other agencies. The CIA is in charge of gathering and analyzing intelligence information outside of the United States. It is also involved in covert actions

Harry S. Truman (1884–1972), the thirty-third president of the United States, established the Central Intelligence Group to operate under the National Intelligence Authority on January 22, 1946. Rear Admiral Sidney W. Souers, USNR, was the first director of central intelligence.

against foreign governments. The CIA reports directly to the president and to the National Security Council.

In the agency's fifty-five-year history, it has sometimes been seen at home and abroad as a maverick government with its own set of rules. The CIA has an unfortunate record of directing coups, rigging elections, and plotting assassinations of foreign leaders. Many of the agency's atrocities were revealed during the 1970s when Congress began to investigate it for conducting secret surveillance on U.S. citizens, in violation of the laws that created the agency.

Today, with the threat of the Soviet Union's influence gone and the end of the Cold War, the CIA has shifted its focus to the Middle East and unstable governments that promote terrorism. The September 11, 2001, terrorist attacks on the World Trade Center in New York City and the Pentagon outside of Washington, D.C., have pushed Congress to give the CIA new legal powers to investigate people living in the United States and abroad who might be involved in terrorist activities.

Chapter One

Evolution of the Agency

Gathering intelligence is the process of using both overt and covert tactics to acquire information about military and political activities of governments or businesses. Governments do this through diplomacy, but in many instances, when they need extremely important information, they use covert, or undercover, operations.

Since its inception, the United States has always practiced some form of secret intelligence gathering. At first, it was primarily during times of war that spies infiltrated enemy territory to uncover sensitive information to help the military plot strategies for winning battles and wars. As the country's military operations became more sophisticated, intelligence-gathering methods grew to include code-breaking units run by the armed services and the State Department. Although this kind of intelligence could expose military and diplomatic activity, it could not uncover information about the politics and the intentions of other governments.

The COI

In 1941, war was spreading throughout Europe and Asia. President Franklin D. Roosevelt sensed that although the United States was not involved in the war, there was a need

In June 1941, American president Franklin D. Roosevelt (1882–1945) appointed William J. Donovan as director of the COI to provide the U.S. government with security information, primarily from Europe. After the Japanese attack on Pearl Harbor in Hawaii, Roosevelt established the Office of Strategic Services (OSS), with Donovan as its director, in June 1942.

to have information about the activities of foreign governments. He established the office of Coordinator of Information (COI), which was responsible for collecting news from around the world as well as gathering intelligence. President Roosevelt's decision to create the COI was a step away from the country's desire to remain isolated from the war in Europe and Asia. Most Americans opposed entering the war and felt that it was better to remain isolated and avoid conflicts.

William Donovan, a former attorney and a highly decorated World War I officer, was chosen to head the COI. In the mid-1930s, with Nazi Germany threatening to invade other European countries, Donovan understood that despite the United States's desire to remain isolated, it would be forced to join in the fight against Hitler's tyranny. Donovan made frequent trips to Europe during this time and became convinced that the United States needed to have better intelligence gathering.

Donovan benefited from trips to Europe, and contacts with political figures proved helpful to him as COI director. The office began with limited knowledge of intelligence gathering and sought advice from other sources. The U.S. military intelligence leaders gave the COI access to their undercover foreign intelligence agents and activities. But the greatest source of help came from Britain's Secret Intelligence Service (SIS).

By 1939, Great Britain was at war with Germany. When the United States created the COI (nearly two years after war broke out in Europe), the government asked Britain's SIS for help in intelligence gathering. In an effort to make an ally of the United States, Britain's SIS set up a training school in Canada for COI recruits and sent agents to be instructors. The SIS also helped to establish the new office by giving the United States secrets from its own intelligence-gathering organization.

The COI adapted British operational intelligence techniques to its own needs and improved on them. Once the COI began to work on its own, it did not want to be considered

William J. Donovan was the founding director of America's OSS, the forerunner of the CIA. He is considered by some to be "the father of American intelligence." Assistant attorney general under President Coolidge, Donovan had been a classmate of Franklin D. Roosevelt's at Columbia University.

subservient to Britain and often was reluctant to provide information to its ally.

The OSS

In June 1942 (six months after the United States entered World War II alongside Allied countries Great Britain and the Soviet Union), Roosevelt signed a presidential order establishing the Office of Strategic Services (OSS). The OSS replaced the COI, and Donovan was named director. The OSS was similar to the COI, except it focused primarily on intelligence gathering and no longer ran the Foreign Information Service, which conducted radio broadcasts.

During World War II, the OSS staged covert paramilitary operations to help weaken the Axis powers of Nazi Germany, Italy, and Japan. Its function was primarily sabotage, espionage, counterespionage, covert missions, and subversions. One of the most effective tools of intelligence gathering for the OSS was research and analysis (R&A). Donovan felt that to win the war, research and analysis would be a critical part of all intelligence gathering.

Highly trained scholars and analysts of the R&A division understood the value of information taken from academic books, journals, newspapers, and magazines. Information from American companies gathered during their overseas trips was also valuable for intelligence gathering. Some of it helped the R&A unit to predict that manpower would be a critical problem for the German war machine. The R&A unit also estimated German U-boat and battle casualties by scrutinizing death tolls in German newspapers.

More than 13,000 men and women worked for the OSS during World War II. Agents entered foreign territory by parachuting in or by being smuggled into countries

In 1941, the U.S. State Department desperately needed help in French North Africa. OSS director Donovan sent a dozen officers to North African ports as "vice consuls," where they assembled intelligence essential to the successful Allied landings (Operation TORCH) in November 1942. This operation earned the fledgling OSS support in Washington, and Donovan was able to build the OSS into a respected and powerful organization.

occupied by the enemy. Once there, they worked closely with underground units.

One of the most effective operations conducted by the OSS was its preparation for the Allied landings in North Africa in 1942. The OSS was able to place agents in North Africa who recorded the movements of German warships and aircraft through the Mediterranean Sea. When American and British troops stormed the beaches of North Africa, OSS agents were waiting to lead them through mine-fields and direct them to their strategic locations.

In 1943, OSS agents, with Donovan's approval and without informing the Joint Chiefs of Staff, broke into the Japanese Embassy in Lisbon, Portugal, to search for documents and codebooks. Agents obtained valuable information. But this covert operation was quickly discovered by the Japanese, and it was devastating to U.S. military intelligence. In early 1942, the U.S. military intelligence had broken the Japanese "Ultra Code," which had enabled them to monitor Japanese military and diplomatic messages throughout the war. As a result of the OSS break-in, the Japanese government changed the entire military code used by its intelligence service.

OSS activities during the war also created a demand for devices and documents that could be used to trick or attack the enemy. Most of the devices created were assembled in the research & development branch (R&D) of the OSS. Products ranged from silenced pistols to "Aunt Jemima," an explosive powder packaged in Chinese flour bags. Tiny cameras and inconspicuous letter drops were devised to assist OSS agents in enemy territory. The agency's companion unit, located in the communications branch, developed wiretap devices, electronic beacons for agents in the field, and portable radios—including the "Joan-Eleanor" system, which allowed agents operating in enemy territory to communicate with other agents.

The system included two small radios. The Eleanor radio featured a directional beam that pointed up to a circling aircraft carrying its sister component, the Joan radio, and a recorder to store messages. Outside the beam, the Eleanor was invisible to ground radio systems that were devised to look for spy communications equipment. The two radios got their names from the OSS practice of assigning female names to projects as a security measure.

The R&D also fabricated legal papers that an agent needed to create a believable identity behind enemy lines, including the latest German- and Japanese-issued ration cards, work passes, and identification cards. Even money was perfectly imitated. These items were passed to agents preparing for missions. The lives of agents who were caught carrying fraudulent cards, money, or passes would be in jeopardy. If found to be spies, they could be put to death.

When the war ended in 1945, President Harry S. Truman disbanded the OSS. Some members in the intelligence community protested, most notably Donovan, but Truman felt there was no longer a need to have an intelligence-gathering organization. There was also a feeling that the public might view maintaining such an organization as too similar to Nazi Germany's Gestapo. Many Americans were afraid that such an agency would ultimately spy on unsuspecting citizens.

Attitudes on intelligence gathering, however, would change shortly after the elimination of the OSS. Although the threat of Nazi Germany was gone, there was another

The CIA and American Conflicts

1941	The office of Coordinator of Information (COI) is formed.
	Japan attacks Pearl Harbor on December 7.
	The United States declares war on Japan and joins World War II.
1942	The Office of Strategic Services is created.
1947	The National Security Act is signed, creating the Central Intelligence Agency.
1950–1953	The Korean War.
1961	The Bay of Pigs.
1961–1972	Vietnam War.
1962	The Cuban Missile Crisis.
1972	Watergate.
1985–1987	Iran-Contra.
September 11, 2001	Terrorist attacks on the World Trade Center and the Pentagon.

threat brewing overseas. The war had bankrupted most of Europe. Many governments were unstable and unable to stop uprisings that broke out within their countries. The result was that many governments fell under the influence of the Soviet Union and its Communist rhetoric.

The National Security Act Creates the CIA

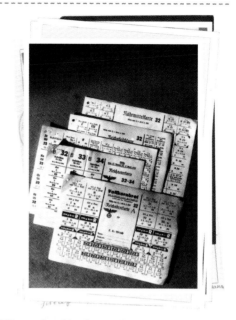

When the Nazis took over countries in their quest for domination, they issued ration cards for food and clothing to the residents. The cards shown above are for meat, eggs, and bread.

Truman, concerned by the Communist threat, finally decided that it would benefit the United States to have a permanent intelligence-gathering organization that could monitor foreign governments and possible threats to the United States. It would report directly to the president. In September 1947, he signed the National Security Act, which created the Central Intelligence Agency (CIA).

Under the guidance of a director of central intelligence, this multifaceted agency was charged with gathering information about "human targets," often without their knowledge. The agency used a variety of methods to get information. Some included electronic eavesdropping, and in many cases intelligence was acquired directly from foreign officials or individuals who had agreed to provide intelligence information in exchange for money or another form of compensation. The CIA also obtained and exchanged information through relationships with foreign intelligence agencies.

Covert action was another intelligence tactic. Covert action is not only the gathering of information; it also refers to any operation in which United States involvement is to remain hidden. A key concept for such actions is the ability of the president to direct the CIA to conduct a covert mission. Covert actions are undertaken when the National Security Council believes that U.S. foreign policy objectives may not become reality through diplomacy, and when military action is considered too extreme. The agency may conduct a special mission to support foreign policy in which the role of the U.S. government is neither apparent nor publicly acknowledged.

Chapter Two

Present-Day Administrative Structure and Methods

At this writing, George J. Tenet is the agency's director of central intelligence (DCI). Sworn in as DCI on July 11, 1997, during the presidency of Bill Clinton, Tenet has been in the intelligence arena for more than a decade.

A native New Yorker, Tenet holds a bachelor of science in foreign services from Georgetown University's School of Foreign Service and a master's degree in international affairs from the School of International Affairs at Columbia University. He is married to A. Stephanie Glakas-Tenet, and they have a son, John Michael.

Before becoming DCI, Tenet was deputy director of central intelligence in 1995. Following the resignation of John Deutch in December 1996, Tenet was named acting DCI. Tenet previously served as special assistant to President Clinton and senior director for intelligence programs at the National Security Council (NSC). While at the National Security Council, he dealt with presidential decision directives on intelligence priorities, security policy coordination, U.S. counterintelligence effectiveness, and U.S. policy on remote sensing space capabilities. He was

On March 19, 2002, CIA director George Tenet testified before the United States Senate Armed Services Committee that Saddam Hussein is a "threat" and is "determined to thwart U.N. sanctions, press ahead with weapons of mass destruction, and resurrect the military force he had before the Gulf War."

also responsible for coordinating interagency activities concerning covert action.

Operation of the CIA

Since the CIA was created more than fifty years ago, the structure of the agency and its mission have remained the same. Very little information is ever revealed about how many people work for the CIA. The agency, however, carefully selects qualified people in nearly all professions. Scientists, engineers, economists, linguists, mathematicians, secretaries, accountants, and computer specialists are among the many professionals who work inside the agency. Much of the CIA's work requires research, careful evaluation, and writing reports that ultimately end up on the desks of the nation's policymakers.

The size of the CIA's budget at one point was considered classified information and wasn't made public. A common misconception is that the agency has unlimited funds. In 1997, the figure for all U.S. government intelligence and intelligence-related activities (of which the CIA is one part) was revealed for the first time. The intelligence budget was $26.6 billion, with the CIA's portion a little more than $3 billion. Since the terrorist attacks on the World Trade Center in New York City and the Pentagon outside of Washington, D.C., on September 11, 2001, President George W. Bush has more than doubled the budget for intelligence activities.

Homeland Security

The terrorist attacks also led to the establishment of the Office of Homeland Security. President Bush named Pennsylvania governor Tom Ridge as its director. For 2003, President Bush has added $37.7 billion to its previous $19 billion budget. Some of these funds go to local governments to support fire departments, police departments, and rescue units. The mission of the new office is to

Tom Ridge, director of Homeland Security, met with United States mayors in an Emergency Safety and Security Summit on October 25, 2001, to discuss a plan for preventing and responding to terrorist attacks.

identify priorities and coordinate efforts for collection and analysis of information relating to terrorism threats and other activities deemed a threat to the country.

Current Intelligence Gathering

William Casey was director of the Central Intelligence Agency from 1981 to 1987. He was a central figure in the Iran-Contra affair in which the United States secretly sold weapons to Iran and gave the profits to the Nicaraguan contra rebels. Casey became ill and died before he could reveal his role in the scandal.

Since the September 11 attacks, the government has been looking back to see how it missed warning signals. In the mid-1980s, a series of terrorist attacks in different parts of the world alerted the U.S. government to the dangers of international terrorism. Vice President George H. W. Bush (father of George W. Bush and the nation's forty-first president) became the chair of a new task force to address the looming problem. Research by the task force at that time revealed that while U.S. government agencies collected information on terrorism, they were not actively disrupting terrorists. In response, then DCI William Casey created the DCI Counterterrorist Center (CTC), whose mission was to help combat terrorism.

The CTC assisted the DCI to coordinate counterterrorist operations within the intelligence community. The CTC collected intelligence information to help agents weaken international terrorist groups and their sponsors. They produced detailed analyses of the groups and governments involved in international terrorism.

The goal of the DCI Counterterrorist Center is to cut off terrorist activities at the earliest possible stage. It was designed to alert government officials of a pending terrorist operation in time to counter the threat. The DCI Counterterrorist Center was supposed to weaken the infrastructures of terrorist groups so that they would be unable to carry out plans. The center was working closely with friendly foreign security and intelligence services through information sharing on terrorist groups and training in terrorist attack prevention.

Tenet told senators in a secret session in the beginning of 2001 that the CIA had helped to foil many terrorist activities. But after U.S. intelligence missed predicting the September 11 attacks, many elected officials continued to question the effectiveness of the CIA.

According to agency officials, the agency has now hired and reassigned hundreds of staffers to the Counterterrorist Center, doubling its size.

The agency is using a new tactic against terrorism, which they call disruption. Designed to prevent terrorist attacks before they happen, this technique has agents continually reviewing lists of names and photographs of terrorist suspects. Agents share information with international law-enforcement services to help prevent attacks around the world. The new mandate for the CIA and its allies is to track down, break up, and destroy international terrorist groups, large and small.

Workers digging out a tent at the U.S.-bombed home of Colonel Muammar Qadhafi in Tripoli, Libya, in 1986. President Ronald Reagan ordered the bombing after learning that Libya took part in an attack on American soldiers in a Berlin discotheque. The bombing, which failed to hit Qadhafi, killed his infant daughter.

Disrupting Terrorist Activities

To disrupt an operation, an agent needs only a small piece of information, usually from an intercepted cell phone call or from a report from a field surveillance team. The CIA might provide evidence to warrant an arrest, such as information that a known terrorist has crossed a border with false papers or illegal weapons. The key to disruption is to stop terrorists before they strike.

There are usually no headlines when there has been a disruptive mission. The CIA keeps its role secret, and the countries that crack down on suspects hide any involvement with the United States for fear of stirring up political

Residents comb through the debris of a damaged building after the U.S. bombing of Iraq in 1993. The United States claimed the bombing was in self-defense as a result of an alleged assassination attempt on former president Bush.

trouble. The CIA sends no formal notice to Congress once a foreign law-enforcement agency, acting on CIA information, swoops in and breaks up a suspected terrorist cell. Secrecy is highly important in conducting a successful act of disruption. In addition, the CIA hides U.S. involvement to avoid the cumbersome congressional reporting requirements that go with CIA-directed covert operations.

Counterterrorism officials rely heavily on disruption tactics because they are one of the very few options that yield good results. Once a terrorist strike occurs, it is often very difficult to find and arrest suspects. Occasionally authorities do locate suspects, but it doesn't happen often. The United States is still trying to find the perpetrators of

A picture of Osama bin Laden released by *Dawn*, a respected Pakistani newspaper, to accompany a November 10, 2001, interview. Bin Laden told his interviewer that he had nuclear and chemical weapons, which he was considering using in response to U.S. attacks on Afghanistan.

the 1998 U.S. Embassy bombings in Africa.

Though U.S. officials often threaten military reprisal against terrorists, they have used the option only four times. This includes the 1986 bombing of two Libyan cities, the 1993 cruise missile strike on Iraq, and the 1998 attack on suspected terrorist strongholds in Sudan and Afghanistan. In 2001, the U.S. attacked Afghanistan with missiles and sent in military ground troops against the Taliban government. The mission in Afghanistan was also meant to capture international terrorist Osama bin Laden, who is considered the mastermind behind the September 11 terrorist attacks, as well as capture members of his terrorist group, Al Qaeda. At this writing, the whereabouts of bin Laden are still unknown.

Human-Rights Issues

The CIA and several other intelligence agencies have been notorious for encouraging (or associating with) people who commit human-rights violations, including torture, ill treatment, disappearances, executions, or similar violations of the laws of war. These crimes may result from a covert operation instigated by the U.S. government, such as a coup d'état. Human-rights violations may be committed by a human intelligence source (also known as an "asset") employed by the agency. For example, when international law enforcers get rough in the process of breaking up a suspected terrorist cell, the CIA has no direct control. Human-rights organizations usually have no way of identifying the role of the CIA. Intelligence agencies also have relationships with their counterparts overseas, many of which may be notorious human-rights violators themselves.

Human-rights violators who are U.S. intelligence sources or assets may feel that the United States approves of their actions. Because the U.S. government continues to work with these people rather than turning them over for prosecution, some human-rights groups believe that the U.S. government encourages criminal activity. By shielding criminals from scrutiny using the "sources and methods" rationale (which argues that sources and methods of obtaining information must be protected), the U.S. government could be considered an accomplice to violations of human rights.

Chapter Three

America at War

At the beginning of the 1900s, the United States was still considered a young nation with a growing military. The country was still recovering from the Civil War, a brutal conflict between the North and the South in which thousands of young men lost their lives. Eventually, the United States turned its attention to expanding its powers past its borders into regions that included Latin America, the Caribbean, and the Pacific.

Filipino-American War (1899–1902)

The Filipino-American War was America's first true colonial war. After defeating Spain in Cuba and in the Philippines in 1898, the United States purchased the Philippines, Puerto Rico, and several other islands from Spain. However, the Filipinos had been fighting a bloody war of independence against Spain since 1896 and had no intention of becoming a colony of another imperialist power. In February 1899, fighting broke out between the occupying American army and the Filipino forces.

By November 1899, the Filipino forces realized that the only way to fight the American troops was by guerrilla warfare. From this point on, the war became a savage, no-holds-barred conflict made up of ambushes, massacres, and retribution. Villages were destroyed, civilians were murdered, and prisoners were tortured and mutilated along with a host of other atrocities. President Theodore Roosevelt finally declared an end to the war on July 4, 1902, but uprisings continued for another decade.

World War I (1917–1918)

When war erupted in Europe in 1914, the United States wanted to remain isolated from the conflict. An isolationist foreign policy was encouraged by Congress's fear about foreign countries having political influence on

Theodore Roosevelt (1858–1919) was president of the United States from 1901 to 1909. Angry at the direction Republican presidential candidate William Taft was taking the country in 1912, Roosevelt became the nominee of the Progressive Party. His candidacy split the Republican Party and put Democratic candidate Woodrow Wilson in office.

U.S. government policies. Despite this effort, the United States entered World War I.

Before 1915, German submarines had a policy of warning ships to allow them time to evacuate passengers before they were attacked. In 1915, however, the passenger ship *Lusitania* was sunk without a warning, killing more than 120 Americans. One year later, German U-boats sank the *Sussex*. The United States was outraged at these violations of its neutral rights at sea. As a result, some Americans, including former president Theodore Roosevelt, running for office once more, wanted the

President Woodrow Wilson believed in peace and hoped that the United States could help broker the end of World War I. When a German U-boat torpedoed and sank the passenger ship *Lusitania* in May 1915, Wilson demanded an apology from Germany, which never came.

country to declare war. Woodrow Wilson was elected president in 1916. As president, he took a strong position on foreign affairs by increasing the size of the military and issuing a warning to Germany that the United States would cut off all ties with the country if attacks continued.

Germany temporarily stopped submarine warfare until 1917, when it announced the continuation of submarine attacks and ended diplomatic relations with the United States. Military strategists predicted certain defeat for the Germans if the United States entered the war. In an attempt to eliminate the threat of American involvement in Europe, Germany tried to involve Mexico and Japan in an attack on the United States with the promise of German assistance after Europe was conquered. A message containing Germany's intent, however, was decoded by the British and sent to America, encouraging the United States to declare war on Germany on April 6, 1917.

World War II (1941–1945)

At 7:55 AM on Sunday, December 7, 1941, the first of two waves of Japanese aircraft began their deadly attack on the U.S. Pacific Fleet at Pearl Harbor on the island of Oahu, Hawaii. Within two hours, 5 battle-ships had been sunk,

President Wilson kept the United States neutral for as long as possible. When British intelligence intercepted a secret German communication in 1917 that promised Mexico United States territory in exchange for supporting Germany, Wilson finally asked Congress for a formal declaration of war. The headline of this paper from April 6, 1917, announces the U.S. declaration of war on Germany.

another 16 damaged, and 188 aircraft destroyed. By chance, three U.S. aircraft carriers, usually stationed at Pearl Harbor but assigned elsewhere on that day, were spared. The attacks killed more than 2,400 Americans, leaving another 1,178 injured. A week later, the United States declared war on Japan and joined the Allied powers of Great Britain and the Soviet Union in their fight against the Axis powers of Germany, Italy, and Japan.

This photo shows the sinking of the USS *Arizona* during the Japanese attack on "battleship row" in Pearl Harbor, Hawaii, on December 7, 1941. U.S. intelligence believed the Japanese would attack the Indies, Malaysia, and perhaps the Philippines. They missed all signs that Pearl Harbor would be a target.

Though the United States entered the war after Japan's sneak attack on Pearl Harbor, the country had been helping Britain to resist Nazi Germany for two years and had been monitoring Japan's aggression in China. After the United States entered, the war lasted for four more years. World War II resulted in the deaths of more than six million Jewish people (at the hands of the Nazis) and millions of soldiers on all sides.

Chapter Four

The Cold War (1950-1991)

After World War II ended, the United States focused its attention on the Soviet Union, which was establishing Communist governments throughout Europe and Asia. This was the beginning of the Cold War.

During the first few years of the Cold War, the conflict between the Communist world and the United States was intense, although it remained peaceful. The United States, determined to prevent the spread of Communism, invested billions of dollars in supporting pro-American governments and developing military alliances. The CIA worked alongside Great Britain's intelligence organizations on a number of covert missions between 1950 and 1991 in an effort to thwart Communism.

The Korean War (1950–1953)

On June 25, 1950, the Cold War suddenly turned red-hot when the Communist government of North Korea (aided by the Chinese) ordered the invasion of South Korea. Its goal was to reunify the Korean peninsula, which had been divided after World War II. The north was under the influence of the Soviet Union, but the south was not.

In this 1950 photo, U.S. troops move into the front lines during the Korean War (1950–1953). After World War II, a republic was established on the southern half of the Korean peninsula, and a Communist-style government was set in the north. The Korean War was a conflict in which U.S. and UN forces defended South Korea from North Korean attacks, which were supported by the Chinese. An agreement was signed in 1953 to end the fighting.

President Truman quickly sent U.S. troops to defend its ally. Throughout the summer of 1950, the United States and the United Nations's member countries attempted to contain the North Korean army.

By the middle of 1951, negotiators began to arrange a truce. But it took two more years to reach a resolution. Negotiations concluded on July 27, 1953. The fighting ended, and each country remained separate. The Cold War, considerably warmed up by the Korean conflict, would maintain its costly existence for nearly four more decades.

Allen Dulles, DCI

The early years of the CIA's history involved the use of covert missions, many led by Allen Dulles, the agency's longest-serving DCI (director of central intelligence). Dulles is considered to have made a major impact on the agency. A member of the OSS, Dulles was appointed to the CIA in 1953. He led the agency in its first few years during the Cold War, as it grew to be the equal of the Soviet Union's KGB.

Active in U.S. espionage service well before World War II, Allen Dulles was a hands-on intelligence officer who helped to create the CIA. He served as its director from 1953 to 1961, during the height of the Cold War, and lost his job after the failed Bay of Pigs invasion in 1961.

Born in Watertown, New York, in 1894, Dulles entered the diplomatic service in 1916, and ten years later earned a law degree from George Washington University. Spending time in Europe in the 1930s, Dulles gained experience gathering intelligence. His knowledge eventually led to his appointment in 1942 as station chief in Berne, Switzerland, for the newly formed OSS. Dulles was able to obtain sensitive information about Nazi Germany for the United States. In 1945, he played a role in negotiations that led to the disbanding of German troops in Italy.

During the height of the Cold War, Dulles gave equal emphasis to the clandestine collection of information as to

The U-2 spy plane, originally developed to help farmers see pictures of their land, could fly at least fifteen thousand feet higher than any other airplane. Its camera, which took the sharpest pictures in the world, was designed by Edwin Land, maker of the Polaroid camera.

involvement in covert activities. Through covert activities, the CIA was instrumental in overthrowing the governments of Iran (1953) and Guatemala (1954). Dulles saw these kinds of events as essential parts of the struggle against Communism, even if they did not always comply with the law.

Dulles's determination to halt the spread of Communism led the CIA to use the U-2 plane for spying in 1955. The plane, which looked like a glider, was equipped with one of the most powerful cameras of the day. The remarkable camera greatly enhanced the CIA's ability to monitor the Soviet Union's activities. Because of U-2 spy missions, the United States was familiar with the Soviet Union's military equipment, biological weapons factories, and nuclear plants.

The CIA flew spy planes over the Soviet Union from 1956 until 1960, when U-2 pilot Gary Powers was shot down and imprisoned. Powers, who was put on trial, was later exchanged for a KGB spy. This incident ended America's use of spy planes over the Soviet Union.

Bay of Pigs (1961)

The spy planes continued to fly missions over other countries. When the Caribbean

President John F. Kennedy (1917–1963) announced to the nation in October 1962 that intelligence information had revealed secret Soviet missile bases in Cuba, ninety miles off Florida.

island of Cuba fell under the rule of Communist dictator Fidel Castro in 1959, the United States became very concerned. Cuba is only ninety miles off the coast of Florida. In 1961, newly-elected president John F. Kennedy wanted to oust Castro from power. To do this, the United States would have to become involved in covert military operations.

The best-known example of the CIA's covert activity directed toward Castro was the failed 1961 Bay of Pigs invasion of Cuba. The plan was to use Cuban refugees to get rid of Castro and his government. However, miscommunications within the CIA and the Kennedy administration about military strategy were blamed for the mission's lack of success. The mission failed because when rebels landed

When President Kennedy saw intelligence photos like this showing Russian missile equipment at the Mariel port facility in Cuba, he demanded that Russian premier Nikita S. Khrushchev dismantle the missile base. He also ordered a naval blockade of Cuba to prevent further construction. Khrushchev's commanders in Cuba were poised to launch their nuclear weapons if the United States invaded. But Khrushchev eventually complied.

on the shore, Castro's army outnumbered them. President Kennedy held Dulles responsible for the failed invasion attempt. Months after the incident, Dulles resigned as DCI.

Cuban Missile Crisis (1962)

A year after the Bay of Pigs invasion, another crisis began to brew on the island. Cuba began to receive shipments of weapons from the Soviet Union. On October 14, 1962, a U-2 flight brought back evidence of a ballistic missile site under construction on the island. The discovery of Russian missiles in Cuba created a crisis of such intensity that many people felt the world was on the brink of a nuclear war. This period was known as the Cuban Missile Crisis, and for the thirteen

In 1962, Soviet premier Nikita Khrushchev wanted to place middle-range missiles in Cuba, only ninety miles from the United States. Ever since the failed Bay of Pigs invasion in 1961, Cuban leader Fidel Castro wanted a way to protect Cuba from future American invasions and so allowed Khrushchev to place missiles there. In this 1964 photo taken in Moscow, Castro and Khrushchev show their solidarity.

days that it lasted, the U. S. armed forces were at their highest state of readiness. On October 22, President Kennedy gave a televised address to the nation telling of the discovery of missile installations by the U-2 flight and the decision to quarantine the island. He also said that any nuclear missile launched from Cuba would be considered an attack on the United States by the Soviet Union. He demanded the Soviets remove all of their weapons from the island.

Kennedy ordered low-level reconnaissance missions to fly over Cuba once every two hours. On October 26, Nikita Khrushchev, leader of the Soviet Union, sent a letter that proposed removing Soviet missiles and personnel if the United States would guarantee that it would not invade Cuba.

The Vietnam War began when the United States supported the French in fighting Communist North Vietnamese forces under Ho Chi Minh for the right to govern Vietnam. But after eight years, the French withdrew. As the war dragged on, costing the United States thousands of casualties and billions of dollars, American opinion about the Vietnam War turned from general approval to general dissatisfaction. Eventually America withdrew, and South Vietnam surrendered to Communist North Vietnam.

The following day the crisis reached its highest level of tension when a U-2 plane was shot down over Cuba. Khrushchev wrote a second letter demanding that the United States remove missiles in Turkey in exchange for the removal of Soviet missiles in Cuba. Kennedy ignored the second letter and responded by accepting the agreement of the first.

Tensions finally began to ease on October 28 when Khrushchev announced that the dismantling of missile installations in Cuba would be documented. He ordered nuclear missiles to be returned to the Soviet Union.

Vietnam (1961–1972)

CIA operations flourished during the war in Vietnam. As part of its covert operations, the agency ran its own air force under the banner of Air America. The CIA was also involved in training Vietnamese soldiers to overthrow the Communists. Many Americans were horrified when they learned that, after training the Vietnamese, the CIA eventually abandoned them to be killed by opposing Communist forces.

Back home, there was growing opposition to the war, which caused President Lyndon B. Johnson to direct DCI Richard Helms to spy on American dissidents. President Johnson felt that, in addition to being un-American, war protesters might be communists or anarchists who wanted to destroy the American government. Helms, who reportedly resisted these pressures, eventually put political activists under surveillance, in direct violation of the CIA charter. This incident was later revealed when burglars, who broke into the Democratic National Committee office, were found to have tools issued by the CIA. Congressional hearings were held to investigate the CIA.

Watergate (1972)

On June 17, 1972, during the U.S. presidential campaign, five men broke into the Watergate apartment-office complex in Washington, D.C. Their aim was to obtain operations information from the headquarter offices of the Democratic National Committee. The five men, who came to be known as the White House Plumbers, were arrested. The burglars carried with them sophisticated espionage equipment used by the CIA, including cameras, lock picks, miniature tear-gas devices, bugging equipment, and walkie-talkies.

When news broke that burglars carrying CIA equipment had been arrested in Washington, Helms realized the agency was in trouble. Because he was unwilling to take blame for the break-in, President Richard Nixon dismissed Helms in 1973. Nixon appointed him ambassador to Iran, but Helms left the post after appearing before the Senate Foreign Relations Committee. He was caught lying in an attempt to protect CIA secrets. Helms was fined $2,000 and was given a suspended two-year prison sentence. The Watergate episode led to major investigation of the CIA as well as to the fall of President Nixon, the first United States president to resign.

On August 9, 1974, as a result of self-incriminating evidence revealing that he had tried to cover up the Watergate burglary, Richard M. Nixon officially resigned as the thirty-seventh president of the United States. This photo shows women reading the *Washington Star-News* the next day.

The CIA in the 1970s

The CIA had mud on its face for several years following the Watergate scandal. When congressional hearings were ordered, it was revealed that the agency had also been conducting surveillance on unsuspecting American citizens. The once-powerful agency was portrayed in books, movies, and on television as a right-wing, Gestapo-like organization with its own set of laws. The agency was seen as an enemy of the American public instead of its protector against subversion, treason, and deadly foreign espionage.

While the CIA was cleared of any involvement in the Watergate scandal, CIA director William E. Colby, shown here in 1975, was asked to assemble a list of CIA "sins." His report came to 693 pages.

Freedom of Information Act

While William Colby was its director (1973–1976), the CIA was subject to the scrutiny of at least seven congressional committees. During this time, Congress established the Freedom of Information Act, which allowed citizens access to information about government agencies. The CIA found itself nearly helpless. Even the most friendly of foreign intelligence agencies, including Britain, Israel, and Germany, were reluctant to help the CIA in fear that the newly established Freedom of Information Act would compromise their own state secrets.

President Jimmy Carter

In 1979, President Jimmy Carter eased some of the restrictions placed on the CIA, allowing its then DCI, Admiral Stansfield Turner (1977–1981), to conduct limited covert operations abroad, including the surveillance of certain U.S. citizens in foreign countries. Carter allowed Turner to carry on clandestine operations without having to inform him. Carter signed the Intelligence Oversight Act in 1980, which restricted the right of Congress to monitor the CIA to the Senate and House Intelligence Committees. Only eight members of Congress would receive special information, which would be released only under extraordinary circumstances. Under the new act, the president had the right to withhold certain information from these congressional leaders.

The CIA in the 1980s

More CIA power and little or no disclosed information on its operations was music to the ears of William J. Casey, the new

Jimmy Carter, thirty-ninth president of the United States, said in his State of the Union address in January 1981, "Continued improvements in our intelligence. . . are essential if we are to cope successfully with the turbulence and uncertainties of today's world."

CIA chief (1981–1987). Appointed by President Ronald Reagan, for whom he had been campaign manager, Casey thrived on covert activities and shared with Congress as little information as possible.

A Time of Growth Under William J. Casey

During Casey's reign, the CIA recaptured its all-powerful image. It received a 25 percent budget increase in 1983 and enlarged its staff, which had been cut by 40 percent during the 1970s.

Under Casey, the CIA built an addition to its headquarters in Langley, Virginia. The complex's new facility is part of the

Oliver North, a decorated platoon leader in the Vietnam War, later worked in the White House, becoming deputy director for Political-Military Affairs under Ronald Reagan. In 1987, hearings about the Iran-Contra scandal were televised, putting North in the spotlight. North admitted that though he had behaved illegally, he had acted out of patriotism.

tightly guarded buildings on more than 280 acres that is estimated to be worth more than $46 million. More than half of the CIA's employees work in Langley, with the rest spread throughout CIA offices in the United States and in American diplomatic centers around the world. Four separate divisions form the workforce of the agency. The Intelligence Division is responsible for gathering information from published sources, such as speeches by diplomats, as well as from secret documents and reports throughout the world. Scientific and technical equipment and problems are handled by the Research Division. The Support Division coordinates the operations of the headquarters staff and field agents, and the Plans Division supervises all covert operations.

The Iran-Contra Scandal

A secret arrangement was made in the 1980s to provide funds to the Nicaraguan contra rebels from profits gained by selling arms to Iran. The Iran-Contra affair was the product of two separate initiatives during the administration of President Ronald Reagan. The first was a commitment to aid the contra rebels who were involved in guerrilla war against the Sandinista government of Nicaragua. The second was to pacify the Iranian government in order to secure the release of American hostages held by pro-Iranian groups in Lebanon, and to influence Iranian foreign policy in a pro-Western direction.

Ronald Reagan, former screen actor and governor of California, served as president of the United States from 1981 to 1989.

With President Reagan's blessing, Casey's CIA supported the Afghanistan rebels against Soviet Union incursion in the 1980s. The CIA provided arms to Iranian paramilitary groups that opposed Ayatollah Khomeini's rigidly religious regime, and it openly supported the insurgents who fought the left-wing government of Nicaragua.

When the Iran-Contra scandal was made public, Oliver North claimed that Casey and the CIA were behind the entire

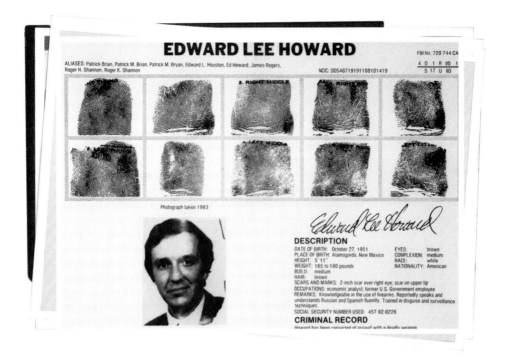

This 1985 poster shows former CIA agent Edward Lee Howard, who was wanted on charges of spying for the Soviet Union. But in a 1995 report to Congress, former CIA analyst John A. Gentry said that some people believed it was the CIA's miserable internal treatment of Howard that drove him to work for the Soviets after he left the agency and that senior officers fabricated Howard's alleged character flaws after they alienated him.

operation. Although Casey was summoned to testify, he died in 1987 before he could confirm or deny the agency's involvement.

The CIA in the 1990s

By the late 1980s, when the agency was headed by former FBI chief William Webster, and into the mid-1990s, the CIA again had its share of problems. It was accused of having brainwashed Canadian citizens thirty years earlier in an effort to compete with brainwashing techniques developed by the Soviet Union, China, and North Korea.

Then in 1994, one of the CIA's worst fears became reality. There was a traitor in its midst. Aldrich Ames, the son of a CIA executive, was exposed as a Soviet spy. Ames was paid more than $2 million by the Soviets for giving them the names of America's best Russian informants, causing the deaths of half a dozen or more men. Arrested and convicted of espionage, Ames, who could have received the death penalty, made a deal to give the American government information in exchange for life imprisonment. His wife got a five-year sentence for being an accomplice.

Other CIA traitors included Edward Lee Howard, who sold secrets to the Russians before fleeing to Moscow. CIA officer William Peter Kampiles sold the Soviets a top-secret manual for a CIA *Spy-in-the-Sky* satellite. CIA analyst Larry Wu-Tai-Chin, who had been born in Beijing, spied for China for thirty years before his 1986 conviction and suicide. None of the damage done by these CIA traitors, however, approached the devastation to the CIA caused by Ames.

Chapter Five

Looking Forward

Some intelligence experts believe the attacks on the World Trade Center and the Pentagon could be the worst intelligence failure in recent U.S. history. Nearly 3,000 people lost their lives and thousands more were injured (more people than the attack on Pearl Harbor). The sense of security the nation once felt was forever wiped away.

The attacks also put intelligence services back into the national spotlight. The National Security Act, which established the CIA, was created in part to prevent another horrific event, such as the Pearl Harbor attack, and envisioned the enemy to be the Soviet Union. The framework for the CIA was created in a different time to deal with different problems. The threat to America's safety no longer comes from the Communist countries but from terrorist organizations, mainly militant religious fanatics, who view the United States as an "evil empire."

The CIA has been busy cultivating relationships with foreign intelligence services that could be helpful in tracking terrorist organizations in the future. Intelligence experts believe the most effective tools for stopping future attacks will come from human intelligence gathering. The agency has shifted spies from foreign bases and is recruiting foreigners within the United States, specifically Arabs and natives of Iran, Iraq, and Afghanistan, to help win the country's war on terrorism.

On September 11, 2001, terrorists crashed two commercial jetliners into the World Trade Center in New York City, destroying both towers. The same morning, a hijacked plane also hit the Pentagon, causing major damage, and a fourth terrorist-controlled plane, which may have been intended for a target in Washington, D.C., crashed in Pennsylvania. American intelligence agencies missed signals that this attack was being planned.

Intelligence experts also believe the CIA will rely heavily on the collection of intelligence through technical means, such as intercepting communications. Human sources, or HUMINT, can provide access to valuable signals intelligence— primarily voice and data communications intelligence. Communications intercepts can validate information provided by a human source. A prerequisite for good human intelligence is to thoroughly understand the sources of terrorism. Much of this kind of information can be obtained from local newspapers in the communities that spawn and protect terrorist organizations. Such analytic information is essential for planning how to penetrate terrorist groups, undertaking covert operations to disrupt terrorist activities and facilities, and collecting information.

To aid the intelligence services and the law enforcement communities, the U.S. Congress has approved antiterrorism legislation that gives these agencies new powers to monitor and detain suspected terrorists.

Key provisions of the legislation include:

■ Using roving wiretaps with only a single warrant, which allows authorities to tap whatever communication device a suspect uses.

■ Making it a crime to harbor a terrorist knowingly.

■ Allowing authorities to detain immigrants for up to seven days if they are suspected of terrorist activities.

■ Giving investigators broader powers to intercept e-mail information.

Terrorism

"Terrorism" is premeditated, politically motivated violence conducted against civilians by splinter groups or self-appointed agents, usually intended to bully or frighten. "International terrorism" means terrorism that involves the territory or the citizens of more than one country. The term "terrorist group" means any group that practices or has significant sub-groups that practice international terrorism.

Civil-rights advocates warn that the new provisions discriminate against immigrants and infringe upon the basic rights of citizens. Despite these concerns, Attorney General John Ashcroft has defended the measures as being effective tools in fighting terrorism.

In 1998, DCI George Tenet addressed CIA employees on the agency's strategic direction. In his address he said, "The threat of terrorism is growing more diverse, complex, and dangerous. It has become easier for small groups to do serious harm with less visibility and warning."

At the time, Tenet said the primary goal of the agency was to strengthen its two fundamental capabilities: clandestine collection and all-source analysis. Clandestine technical operations have consistently revealed valuable intelligence. Since the September 11, 2001, terrorist attacks in the United States, the agency continues to build its field strength by increasing the number of its operations officers

In this photo from October 8, 2001, Attorney General John Ashcroft is at a briefing for reporters at the Justice Department in Washington. He is announcing the FBI investigation into whether terrorism or criminal activity was responsible for the presence of the anthrax bacteria in two Florida men.

and increasing the number of its stations and bases in foreign countries.

The CIA played a central role in designing and executing the American battle plan in Afghanistan shortly after the September 11 attacks, which relied heavily on a combination of intelligence and military operations. The agency also expanded its war-fighting role by using field officers and specialized weapons, such as the unmanned missile-firing *Predator* spy plane, to support American forces in combat.

The CIA has renewed its interest in developing improved espionage technologies. Some expect the CIA to invest heavily in secret scientific projects, hoping to regain the inventive role it played during the Cold War, when it pioneered the development of spy satellites.

Rule Changes at the CIA

There is also heightened debate about some of the controversial rules that govern CIA operations. The first issue is how CIA case officers in the field may recruit agents. In 1995, the CIA established a policy requiring the Directorate of Operations headquarters to approve the recruitment of sources believed to have serious criminal or abusive human-rights records. Officials can apply a balancing test: Is the potential gain from information obtained worth the cost of doing business with a person who may be a murderer or a rapist?

Some believe this rule has constrained case officers from recruiting agents inside terrorist groups, making it harder to predict and stop terrorist acts. Senior CIA officials maintain that the rule has reduced neither the quality nor the quantity of counterterrorism intelligence. Congress recently enacted a "sense of the Congress" provision, as part of the new antiterrorism law, encouraging intelligence officers to "make every effort" to "establish relationships" with such individuals.

Another change in rules concerns wiretaps. Visitors in the United States and U.S. citizens, particularly if they work for U.S. corporations set up as front organizations associated with suspected terrorist groups, will now be subject to possible wiretapping. At this writing, Congress also loosened the reins on courts, allowing them to authorize warrants for national security wiretaps and searches. The intelligence community

President George W. Bush signs the USA Patriot Act of 2001 into law on October 26, 2001. Behind him are Representative Michael Moxley (Ohio), Senator Orrin Hatch (Utah), Senator Patrick Leahy (Vermont), Senator Harry Reid (Nevada), and Representative F. James Sensenbrenner (Wisconsin). The controversial legislation gives police authority to search homes, eavesdrop on phone calls and e-mail, and perform other types of surveillance. It is considered a threat to American civil liberties by critics and vital to U.S. security by supporters.

says that it needs access to telecommunications and databases to track the movements of suspected terrorists operating in the United States. In addition, corporations, including banks and airlines, will now be asked or required to help authorities trace suspected terrorists.

Future Challenges and Goals

Experts believe that the future mission of U.S. intelligence will be to destroy terrorist cells as well as facilities that may be used to produce or store weapons of mass destruction.

Experts also say that there is a better chance of creating effective counterterrorism results if the U.S. military, the CIA, and the FBI are able to work together. But the different approval and reporting procedures of these organizations may be severely challenged. It has been suggested that a new planning staff be created under the leadership of the secretary of defense. In addition, current law requires all CIA covert action be subject to a presidential finding and a report to Congress.

The United States will probably maintain its edge in information and weapons technology, and in military might, during the next decade. Of increasing importance to holding its position of world leadership will be the strength of its economy, the effectiveness of its educational system, and its investment in research and development.

Experts also envision the U.S. military working with American technology specialists to give the United States an expanded lead in conventional war-fighting capabilities.

However, some potential adversaries will seek to threaten U.S. homeland security by using unconventional means. The United States's national infrastructure—communications, transportation, financial industry, energy networks—is considered vulnerable to disruption by physical and electronic attacks as well as by cyber-attacks.

Another challenge the CIA faces is the retirement of senior intelligence agents. As the agency hires hundreds of new intelligence officers, Director Tenet must be careful to recruit people well suited for the responsibilities that come with operating on behalf of the United States in some of the world's most treacherous places. Tenet has said that by 2005, more than 30 percent of the CIA workforce will have been on the job for five years or less. The influx of new employees and the retirement of veterans could leave the agency without an adequate number of battle-tested leaders. That makes it important for Tenet to promote people with good values. It takes years to train a case officer to operate overseas in a hostile environment as well as to recruit and supervise human resources.

Glossary

ballistic missile A missile that is guided in the first part of its flight but falls freely as it approaches its target.

clandestine Conducted with secrecy; withdrawn from public notice; kept secret.

classified Designated as confidential, secret, or top secret.

counterespionage Espionage undertaken to detect and counteract enemy espionage; spying on the spy.

coup d' état The sudden overthrow of a government, usually by a small group of persons in or previously in positions of authority.

covert action Secretive tactics used to gather information about an unsuspecting target.

diplomacy The art and practice of conducting negotiations between nations (particularly in securing treaties), including the methods and forms usually employed.

disseminate To scatter widely; to spread abroad; to distribute.

espionage The act or practice of spying or of using spies to obtain secret information from another government or a business competitor.

Gestapo The German internal security police organized under the Nazi regime, known for its terrorist methods directed against people suspected of treason or questionable loyalty, or considered dangerous because of their race.

infiltrate   To pass gradually and secretly into enemy-held territory for purposes of espionage or takeover.

isolationism   A national policy of avoiding political or economic relations with other countries.

KGB   The intelligence and internal security agency of the former Soviet Union.

overt   Open and observable; not hidden, concealed, or secret.

paramilitary   Relating to a group of civilians organized to function like a military unit; a group of civilians organized in a military fashion (especially to operate in place of or to assist regular army troops).

sabotage   Treacherous action to defeat or hinder a cause or an endeavor; deliberate subversion.

subversions   Acts of overturning, or states of being overturned; utter destruction, as subversions of governments.

For More Information

Central Intelligence Agency
Office of Public Affairs
Washington, DC 20505
(703) 482-0623
Web site: http://www.cia.gov

The George Bush Presidential Library and Museum
1000 George Bush Drive West
College Station, TX 77845
(979) 260-9552
Web site: http://bushlibrary.tamu.edu

The International Spy Museum
800 F Street NW
Washington, DC 20004
(866) SPYMUSEUM or (202) EYE-SPY-U
Web site: http://www.spymuseum.org

The Richard Nixon Library and Birthplace
18001 Yorba Linda Boulevard
Yorba Linda, CA 92886
(714) 993-5075
Web site: http://www.nixonfoundation.org/index.shtml

Web Sites

Due to the changing nature of Internet links, the Rosen Publishing Group, Inc., has developed an online list of Web sites related to the subject of this book. This site is updated regularly. Please use this link to access the list:

http://www.rosenlinks.com/iwmfia/cia/

For Further Reading

Allen, Thomas B., and Norman Polmar. *Spy Book: The Encyclopedia of Espionage*. New York: Random House, 1998.

Ciment, James. *The Young People's History of the United States*. New York: Barnes & Noble Books, 1998.

Fridell, Ron. *Spying: The Modern World of Espionage*. Breckenridge, CO: Twenty-First Century Books, 2002.

Hakim, Joy. *From Colonies to Country*. New York: Oxford University Press, 1998.

Platt, Richard. *Eyewitness: Spy*. New York: DK Publishing, 2000.

Platt, Richard. *Spies!* New York: DK Publishing, 2000.

Tanaka, Shelley. *Attack on Pearl Harbor: The True Story of the Day America Entered World War II*. New York: Hyperion Books for Children, 2000.

Bibliography

Auster, Bruce B., and Brian Duffy. "In from the Cold: The CIA's New Role." *U.S. News & World Report*, November 2, 1998.

Central Intelligence Agency. "Frequently Asked Questions about the CIA." Retrieved February 2002 (http://www.cia.gov).

Cline, Ray. *The CIA: Reality vs. Myth: The Evolution of the Agency from Roosevelt to Reagan*. Washington, DC: Acropolis Books, 1982.

Encyclopedia.Com. Korean War; Vietnam War; Iran-Contra. Retrieved March 2002 (http://www.encyclopedia.com).

Katz, Barry M. *Research and Analysis in the Office of Strategic Services, 1942–1945*. Cambridge, Massachusetts: Harvard University Press, 1989.

Ranelagh, John. *The Agency: The Rise and Decline of the CIA*. New York: Simon & Schuster, 1986.

Smith, Richard Harris. *OSS: The Secret History of America's First Central Intelligence Agency*. Berkeley, California: University of California Press, 1972.

Staff Writers. "Clean State: More Candor About Past Would Benefit the CIA." *Houston Chronicle*, November 9, 1998.

Tenet, George J. "George J. Tenet Biography." Retrieved February and March 2002 (http://www.cia.gov/cia/information/tenet/html).

Index

Credits

About the Author

Janet Hines, a journalist, lives in New York.

Photo Credits

Cover © Roger Ressmeyer/Corbis; p. 5 © Corbis; pp. 6, 8, 15, 27, 28, 30, 32, 34, 35, 37, 43 © Hulton/Archive/Getty Images, Inc.; pp. 9, 11, 29, 42, 44, 46 © Bettmann/Corbis; pp. 18, 22, 24, 49 © Reuters NewMedia, Inc./Corbis; p. 19 © AFP Photo/Shawn Thew/Corbis; pp. 20, 36, 45 © Corbis; p. 23 © Peter Turnley/Corbis; p. 33 © The Bettmann Archive/Corbis; pp. 38, 52, 54 © AP/Wide World Photos; p. 41 © Owen Franken/Corbis.

Layout and Design

Thomas Forget

Editor

Jill Jarnow